GW00384895

I Believe in You

summersdale

I BELIEVE IN YOU

Copyright © Summersdale Publishers Ltd, 2023

Compiled by Maria Medeiros

An Hachette UK Company
www.hachette.co.uk

Summersdale Publishers Ltd
Part of Octopus Publishing Group Limited
Carmelite House
50 Victoria Embankment
LONDON
EC4Y 0DZ
UK

www.summersdale.com

Printed and bound in Poland

ISBN: 978-1-80007-698-3

To..

From..

Believe in yourself. You are braver than you think, more talented than you know, and capable of more than you imagine.

Roy T. Bennett

You are what you believe yourself to be.

Paulo Coelho

You glow differently when you believe in yourself

Your victory is right around the corner. Never give up.

Nicki Minaj

To accomplish great things, we must not only act, but also dream; not only plan but also believe.

Anatole France

It's been pretty incredible to see what happens when you start believing you are enough.

Meghan, Duchess of Sussex

Believe in yourself and you will be unstoppable

NEVER DULL YOUR SHINE FOR SOMEBODY ELSE.

Tyra Banks

Any transition
is easier if you
believe in yourself
and your talent.

Priyanka Chopra

Every
achievement
starts with
the decision
to try and the
confidence
to act

The one thing
you've gotta
do is… do the
best you can do,
no matter what
the given situation.

James Corden

If you believe in yourself anything is possible.

Miley Cyrus

What lies behind you and what lies in front of you, pales in comparison to what lies inside of you.

Ralph Waldo Emerson

IF YOU NEED
SOMEBODY
TO BELIEVE
IN – START
WITH
YOURSELF

If there's one thing
I'm willing to bet
on, it's myself.

Beyoncé

Always be yourself, express yourself, have faith in yourself.

Bruce Lee

EVERYTHING
THAT YOU
ARE IS
ENOUGH

**May all
your vibes
say: I got this.**

Cleo Wade

You've always got to believe in the positives.

Lewis Hamilton

It's the moment you think you can't, that you can.

Celine Dion

YOU HAVE
TO BELIEVE
IN ORDER TO
ACHIEVE

OPTIMISM IS THE FAITH THAT LEADS TO ACHIEVEMENT.

Helen Keller

You're braver
than you believe,
stronger than
you seem, and
smarter than
you think.

A. A. Milne

Live life on your terms and never apologize for it

Once you believe
in yourself, and
you put your mind
to something,
you can do it.

Simone Biles

There are ups and downs, but whatever happens, you have to trust and believe in yourself.

Luka Modrić

Always believe
in yourself and
keep going.

Dean Cain

Confidence
is fuelled
by belief
in yourself
instead of
validation
from others

I am the sole author of the dictionary that defines me.

Zadie Smith

You have to trust your own journey and your strengths and believe in yourself.

Kat Graham

Turn a "can't"
into a "can"
and turn
your dreams
into plans

Once you choose hope, anything's possible.

Christopher Reeve

Even if you don't feel like you have it in you, it's in you.

Teyonah Parris

You alone are enough. You have nothing to prove to anybody.

Maya Angelou

KNOW YOURSELF, BELIEVE YOURSELF, CHOOSE YOURSELF

YOU ARE THE HERO OF YOUR OWN STORY.

Joseph Campbell

Believe in yourself, and find ways to express yourself, and find the discipline to keep growing.

Michael Feinstein

DECIDE WHO YOU WANT TO BE AND START SHOWING UP AS THAT PERSON

You define your
own life. Don't let
other people write
your script.

Oprah Winfrey

You have to believe in yourself or you won't get anywhere.

James DeGale

Be yourself; everyone else is already taken.

Oscar Wilde

YOUR WORTH IS NON-NEGOTIABLE

Believe you
can and you're
halfway there.

Theodore Roosevelt

You change the world by being yourself.

Yoko Ono

You are the creator of your own destiny

You are not a
drop in the ocean.
You are the entire
ocean in a drop.

Rumi

Believe in yourself, listen to your gut, and do what you love.

Dylan Lauren

Don't be afraid to be ambitious about your goals. Hard work never stops. Neither should your dreams.

Dwayne Johnson

Believe you can and you will

THERE'S NO LIMIT TO WHAT I CAN DO.

Leylah Fernandez

Human potential is the only limitless resource we have in this world.

Carly Fiorina

Your opinion
of you is all
that matters

You must
believe
in yourself.

Cher

It's all about
having that inner
confidence.

Jennifer Aniston

Live your beliefs and you can turn the world around.

Henry David Thoreau

You have
more inner
resilience
than you
realize

One step at a
time, I get to
make positive
choices to fulfill
my dreams.

Deena Kastor

I am my own experiment. I am my own work of art.

Madonna

The
impossible
becomes
possible
when you
wholeheartedly
believe
in you

I don't think there is anything wrong with just quietly believing in yourself.

Jessica Ennis-Hill

When people
don't believe
in you, you have
to believe in
yourself.

Pierce Brosnan

All you need
is the plan,
the road map
and the courage
to press on to
your destination.

Earl Nightingale

Be grateful for what you have achieved and fearless for what you want

Dreams don't have to just be dreams. You can make it a reality.

Naomi Osaka

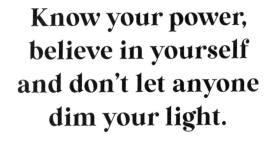

Know your power, believe in yourself and don't let anyone dim your light.

Leigh-Anne Pinnock

Celebrate every win, no matter how small – you are doing better than you think

YOU NEED TO BELIEVE IN YOURSELF AND WHAT YOU DO. BE TENACIOUS AND GENUINE.

Christian Louboutin

It's never too
late to take a
leap of faith
and see what
will happen.

Jane Fonda

Why fit in
when you
were born to
stand out?

Dr. Seuss

BE
UNAPOLOGETICALLY
YOU

Always be a
first-rate
version
of yourself,
instead of
a second-rate
version of
somebody else.

Judy Garland

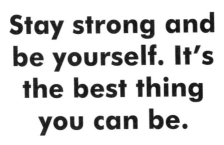

Stay strong and be yourself. It's the best thing you can be.

Cara Delevingne

TRUST
THE NEXT
CHAPTER,
BECAUSE
YOU ARE THE
AUTHOR

If you are your regular, authentic, confident self, then you can push to do whatever you want.

Marsai Martin

Find out who
you are and do
it on purpose.

Dolly Parton

If you're presenting yourself with confidence, you can pull off pretty much anything.

Katy Perry

YOU
HAVE THE
CAPABILITY
TO BRING
ALL YOUR
HOPES INTO
FRUITION

Believe in your heart what you know to be true about yourself.

Mary J. Blige

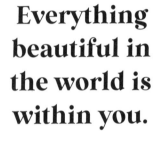

Everything beautiful in the world is within you.

Russell Brand

No one can
do what you
do, the way
you do –
that's your
superpower

I believe in
being strong
when everything
seems to be
going wrong.

Audrey Hepburn

Push your boundaries beyond the ordinary: be that "extra" in "extraordinary".

Roy T. Bennett

BELIEVE IN YOURSELF WHEN NO ONE ELSE DOES. THAT MAKES YOU A WINNER RIGHT THERE.

Venus Williams

Take control of the narrative — go get whatever sets your soul on fire

Owning who you are
and knowing what
you want is the
only sure path
to affirmation.

Ashley Graham

You are more
powerful than
you know.

Melissa Etheridge

SOMETIMES YOU JUST NEED TO BE BRAVE ENOUGH TO TAKE THE NEXT STEP, NOT CLIMB THE WHOLE STAIRCASE

I will not let anyone scare me out of my full potential.

Nicki Minaj

The potential for greatness lives within each of us.

Wilma Rudolph

Believe in
yourself and
stop trying to
convince others.

James de la Vega

YOU ARE
LOVED,
YOU ARE
VALUED,
YOU ARE
WORTHY

You can have all the tools in the world but if you don't genuinely believe in yourself, it's useless.

Ken Jeong

I WAS ALWAYS LOOKING OUTSIDE MYSELF FOR STRENGTH AND CONFIDENCE BUT IT COMES FROM WITHIN. IT IS THERE ALL THE TIME.

Anna Freud

UPGRADE
YOUR
MINDSET
TO MATCH
YOUR
DESTINY

**Be yourself.
The world
worships
the original.**

Ingrid Bergman

Find out who you are and be that person.

Ellen DeGeneres

I believe in
the impossible
because no one
else does.

Florence Griffith Joyner

The places
you are going
to are more
important
than the
places you
have been

You can do
anything you
decide to do.

Amelia Earhart

If my mind can conceive it, and my heart can believe it – then I can achieve it.

Muhammad Ali

Show up
for yourself
and choose
progress not
perfection

Never give up,
for that is just
the place and
time that the
tide will turn.

Harriet Beecher Stowe

Whatever you
want to do,
do it now.
There are
only so many
tomorrows.

Michael Landon

WHEN IT COMES TO LUCK, YOU MAKE YOUR OWN.

Bruce Springsteen

Be your
own muse

Success in any endeavour depends on the degree to which it is an expression of your true self.

Ralph Marston

You will not determine my story. I will.

Amy Schumer

BE THE PERSON YOU LOOK UP TO

To love oneself is the beginning of a lifelong romance.

Oscar Wilde

Be bold,
be brave
enough to be
your true self.

Queen Latifah

Believe in
yourself,
go after your
dreams, and
don't let
anyone put
you in a box.

Daya

Believe
and trust
in yourself
and you
can achieve
anything

Just don't give
up trying to do
what you really
want to do. Where
there is love and
inspiration, I
don't think you
can go wrong.

Ella Fitzgerald

Believe in others.
Believe in yourself.
Believe in your
dreams. If you
don't, who will?

Jon Bon Jovi

Even a
tiny win is
progress –
keep
believing

Whether you think you can, or think you can't – you're right.

Henry Ford

I am knowledgeable enough to do this. I am prepared enough to do this. I am mature enough to do this. I am brave enough to do this.

Alexandra Ocasio-Cortez

Create the
highest, grandest
vision possible for
your life, because
you become what
you believe.

Oprah Winfrey

Set goals
that liberate
your energy
and inspire
your soul

Believe in your dreams. They were given to you for a reason.

Katrina Mayer

WE ARE
WHAT WE
BELIEVE
WE ARE.

C. S. Lewis

ALL YOUR
DREAMS
CAN COME
TRUE IF YOU
HAVE THE
COURAGE
TO PURSUE
THEM

If you believe
it will work
out, you'll see
opportunities.
If you believe
it won't, you will
see obstacles.

Wayne Dyer

Life isn't about finding yourself. Life is about creating yourself.

George Bernard Shaw

You can be
everything.
You can be the
infinite amount
of things that
people are.

Kesha

DREAM IT,
BELIEVE IT,
ACHIEVE IT

Believe in yourself, take on your challenges, dig deep within yourself to conquer fears.

Chantal Sutherland

The people who
are crazy enough
to think they can
change the world
are the ones
who do.

Steve Jobs

BELIEVE YOU
DESERVE
IT AND THE
UNIVERSE
WILL
SERVE IT

Winning and losing isn't everything. Sometimes the journey is just as important as the outcome.

Alex Morgan

Be so good they can't ignore you.

Steve Martin

If you believe you can get there, then one day you will.

João Moutinho

YOU DON'T
NEED
ANYONE TO
BELIEVE IN
YOU FOR
YOU TO
BELIEVE IN
YOURSELF

I will not lose, for even in defeat, there's a valuable lesson learned, so it evens it up for me.

Jay-Z

THERE IS ALWAYS LIGHT. IF ONLY WE'RE BRAVE ENOUGH TO SEE IT. IF ONLY WE'RE BRAVE ENOUGH TO BE IT.

Amanda Gorman

Never let success go to your head or failure go to your heart

Act as
if what you
do makes a
difference.
It does.

William James

They will always
tell you that
you can't do what
you want to do,
but you can do
what you want to
do. You just have
to believe in
yourself.

Bob Marley

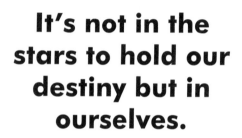

It's not in the stars to hold our destiny but in ourselves.

William Shakespeare

The best thing you will ever do is believe in you

Be messy and
complicated
and afraid
and show
up anyways.

Glennon Doyle

I found that ultimately, if you truly pour your heart into what you believe in... amazing things can and will happen.

Emma Watson

You are the artist of your own life — don't hand the paintbrush to anyone else

Believe in
yourself and
try as much
as possible to
do everything
you do from
a place
of love.

Michael Mando

I just want to remind people that you know yourself better than anybody else and if you don't believe in yourself, then who will?

Camille Kostek

Be yourself, do your own thing and work hard.

Will Smith

Always believe something wonderful is about to happen

WHEN YOU HAVE A DREAM, YOU'VE GOT TO GRAB IT AND NEVER LET GO.

Carol Burnett

The minute you learn to love yourself, you won't want to be anyone else.

Rihanna

ONCE YOU
OPEN YOUR
MIND, THE
POSSIBILITIES
ARE ENDLESS

Believe anything is possible and then work like hell to make it happen.

Julianna Margulies

You have to
believe in yourself.
You need to have
the audacity
to be great.

Rosie Perez

You must love yourself internally to glow externally.

Hannah Bronfman

Success is no
accident. It is
hard work,
perseverance,
learning, studying,
sacrifice and,
most of all,
love of what
you are doing.

Pelé

Nothing is impossible. The word itself says "I'm possible".

Audrey Hepburn

Believe your voice is important and your dreams matter

If you're interested in finding out more about our books, find us on Facebook at Summersdale Publishers, on Twitter at @Summersdale and on Instagram at @summersdalebooks

www.summersdale.com